HOW TO SUCCEED IN CONSTRUCTION

CONSTRUCTION

50 WAYS TO BE A BETTER CARPENTER

How to Succeed in Construction

Construction

50 Ways to be a Better Carpenter

Written by:
Brantley Max

How to Succeed in Construction by Brantley
Max. Published by LH Rue Publishing

© 2020 Brantley Max

Cover by Brantley Max

ISBN: 978-1-7344556-1-8

Introduction

At the time of this writing, the construction industry is experiencing a major labor shortage. Thousands of construction jobs are going unfilled every single day. I read an article recently about a multi-story building sitting unfinished because the general contractor was unable to find enough skilled workers to work on it. The skills gap is affecting every facet of the industry from commercial to residential. A skills gap is the imbalance between jobs available and people skilled enough to fill those jobs. So why is this?

There are many reasons:

- The emphasis on four-year degrees. "Go to college, go to

college", was the message burned in the in the heads of children in schools all across the country. Construction industry jobs were presented as "less desirable". The allure of college and the salaries of jobs like computer programmer were just too enticing. Misconceptions ran amuck.

- The aging workforce. The sheer number of baby boomers set to retire is astounding. Some 36,500,000 workers are approaching retirement age in the next ten years. These workers leave behind many specialized positions with fewer workers to step in and take over.

- Money. As school districts grew and budgets were cut, many programs were placed on the chopping block. Trade programs, apprenticeships, and 2-year vocational schools were the first to go. Children simply chose other paths with these programs no longer an option.

- The economy. Construction is booming! It doesn't appear to be slowing down in the foreseeable future. As more projects become available to bid, more workers are needed to work on these projects. Demand is outpacing supply, with ranges from 60% to 90% of construction companies reporting they have had trouble filling job vacancies.

What does that mean for you? It means that there is no better time than now to get into the skilled trades. To entice workers to work for them, companies have been raising salaries and increasing opportunities for vertical growth. There are skilled carpenters making $80,000 to $110,000! This can easily be you. College isn't for everyone but that doesn't mean you can't enter a career field ripe with opportunities.

When I was starting out in the field I wanted to learn as much as I could. Books on the topic of getting started in construction were hard to find. There were textbooks with boring information on carpentry, but that's not what I was looking for. I wanted practical advice; stuff I didn't have to feel weird about asking my coworkers. Some guys were terrific and were more than happy to pass on their knowledge. Other guys were not as helpful. This book is about the information I was seeking as a young apprentice, starting my journey in construction. Practical advice that would help me excel. If this is what you are looking for, this book is for you. I have been in the construction industry for 25 years. I started as a carpenter apprentice, then worked my way through being a journeyman carpenter, foreman, area supervisor, and construction manager. I moved through all these positions without a college degree. You can too! I have assembled 50 ways in which to help you on your journey.

NUMBER 1

Show Up!

None of the tips and tricks in this book are in order EXCEPT number one and number two. These are extremely important in your success in the construction industry. SHOW UP! Go to work every day. Things will come up and you will have to miss days. Trust me, I have four kids so I understand, but otherwise, show up. Constructions projects almost always have deadlines. Things need to happen and usually by a certain date. In order for that to happen all the pieces and parts need to be in place. Let's say you are putting in windows on the side of a six-story building. Your employer has rented a lift and sent a couple guys to install. If one of the guys doesn't show up, not much can happen like it was supposed to. Your office will then have to scramble to get another guy from another project and will waste valuable install time to make this happen. If you are someone who likes to take days off work once a week because you stayed out too late drinking the night before or your car "breaks" down constantly, this is not the profession for you. You will quickly gain a reputation as being unreliable. This will translate in to you getting "laid off" (which is the construction industry's way of letting you go). The less you work the less money you will make and the harder it will be for you to succeed. Showing up and being someone a contractor can rely on is huge. This alone could open doors for you. We've all heard of people who have hired contractors to come do work for them and then no one ever showed up. This is a problem in the industry. Do your part and show up!

NUMBER 2

Be Early

Get to work early. I cannot stress this enough. If starting time is 7am and you show up at 7am, you're late! A 7am starting time means you should be swinging a hammer at 7am. At minimum you should have your tools out of the gang box and be ready for instruction. This advice along with tip #1 are critical. Good carpenters show up early. I know for a fact that being on the jobsite every morning when my boss pulled in had positive results. I had bosses tell me as much.

A good starting point would be to show up at least 30 minutes early.

You can give yourself a few minutes to breathe and drink your coffee. Then get out of your truck and talk to the other guys. This period of time before you start work for the day can be invaluable for learning about your boss, the company, or even the expectations for the day. People are generally easier to talk with in the morning before the stress of the project starts to hit. You will also hear about the "other" apprentice or journeyman and how he or she is always late, does this and that wrong, and doesn't do something the way your boss wants it done. Take mental notes. You will be in a better position to stick around and be the apprentice or worker the other guys choose over the other carpenters. Again, show up early. This is critical.

NUMBER 3

Buy Good Boots

You will walk.... ALOT! Even on small projects the amount of walking can be immense. Unfortunately, I only figured this out once my feet started hurting. One day years ago, my feet hurt so bad I started researching new boots to try to help and it turns out, your footwear is important. Wearing poor quality boots is putting unnecessary wear and tear on your body. I use to find the cheapest pair of boots I could find at the local Kmart, would pay my $30 and move on. My legs and feet hurt for years. I know it can seem like a struggle or an extravagance to pay upwards of $150 for boots, but it's worth it.

I worked for a casework contractor for a while and we always unloaded our own trucks. We didn't unload pickup trucks but large 53' Semi-trucks. We would usually distribute into a large facility like a new high school or K-12 building. I felt like I was doing a ton of walking especially on unload days. I purchased a new Fitbit exercise band to track my steps. I routinely logged 20,000 steps in a day. One day I hit over 30,000! You are doing yourself a disservice if you are wearing poor quality footwear. Spend the extra money!

Many carpenters swear by Redwings. They have individual stores all over cities across the country. The pairs I had were better than my $30 Kmart boots but I never fell in love with them like the other guys. I found a pair of Carhartt boots that ran about $150 that ended up being my go-to boot. Every foot is different and there will be some trial and error, but you can expect to replace your boots at least once a year, sometimes more. Find what works for you. You'll thank me later.

NUMBER 4

Don't Show Up without a Toolbelt

This is self-explanatory. When I started out in the trades, I had a boss who screamed at everyone to wear their toolbelt. It didn't matter what they were doing. Even if you were sweeping the floor, he still wanted you to wear your toolbelt. He was infamous for this and many unhappy comments were muttered behind his back. It wasn't until years later when I went to work for some guys that used to work for him but had started their own business, did I start to look at this in a different way. My new boss mentioned to me how much they hated the toolbelt rule when they worked for him, but how he and his business partner now understood it. Stopping work flow to go and grab a tool out of the gang box is a major time killer. Having a helper constantly ask to borrow this or that is also annoying. Toolbelts were invented out of necessity, not for fun. Showing up without a toolbelt can turn off an employer before you ever get to show how good of a worker you are. Don't make this mistake!

There are many different theories on what the best toolbelt is and how you should organize your tools. These vary from carpenter to carpenter. As you gain experience and get out in the field you will learn what works best for you. If you admire a guy who seems to carry everything and can access it even with a load of lumber in his hands, pay attention and see if his set-up might work for you. One piece of advice I might add; get a belt with shoulder straps/suspenders. Your lower back will thank you.

NUMBER 5

Use the Right Tool for the Job

If you don't have the right tool for the job, you'll use the tool that you have. We've all hammered a nail with a wrench or used our cordless drill to pry apart two pieces of wood, but this isn't the best route to take. Before you begin a project take inventory of what you will need to do the job effectively and safely. I once used the wrong screws to screw off drywall on an entire floor of a high-rise building office remodel. As the finishers were going through and putting on the first coat of mud, they found that all the screws were loose along with a bunch of the drywall. The "atta-boy" I received for hurrying through and getting everything screwed off quickly turned into "you're a dumbass"! My boss was furious and I had to go back through, dig all the wrong screws out, and put the correct ones in. This slowed down progress, cost unnecessary money and made me feel like an idiot. It took months for me to live this one down. Avoid this at all costs. If you feel you need something to do a job appropriately, ask. If you are using the wrong tool for the job, mistakes are bound to happen. You do not want to be the cause of mistakes. If something doesn't seem right, look into it, it might not be.

NUMBER 6

Work Like your Boss is Watching

I have worked with many carpenters over the years who work well when the boss is there checking in, but as soon as he leaves, they "lay down". They literally watched for him to leave out the window. As soon as he did, they sat down on a bucket or checked their phones. Don't follow in these footsteps. I admit that on occasion I have done this and although I got away with it a few times, there were times when I didn't. I swear there's universal intervention at play. If you start goofing off, the boss will somehow ALWAYS show up at that time. I remember one boss in particular who seemed to always show up at the "wrong" time. I would be digging a trench or pulling up old carpet and would stop to sit down for a minute, look up and there he was, staring at me. I would start explaining that I had only stopped for a second and even when that was true, I could tell he thought I was being lazy. Now I know there will be times when you do need to stop for a second, that's ok, but then get back to work. If your boss routinely "catches" you working, you will make it on the list of favorite employees and set yourself up on the path to promotion. I know this to be true even in my current position. I work with another project manager who always talking to me about one of our carpenters who is always working when he stops by unannounced. He is currently working on making him supervisor over multiple projects. This promotion comes with a truck and more money! Work like your boss is watching and you'll never need to worry about when your boss might show up, you'll already be showing him your best self.

NUMBER 7

Be Safe

There is no project important enough to work in such a way to put your safety in jeopardy. I'm as serious as I can possibly be when I say work safe. Wear your hard hat, wear your safety glasses, and wear your fall protection. Construction can be dangerous. One little mishap can mean not going home to your family. I have witnessed some pretty gruesome accidents and some of those could have been avoided had people worn their Personal Protective Equipment (PPE). Construction suffers from a "to cool for school" attitude towards safety. Guys will try to make you feel less "manly" for practicing safety. They will make fun of you or act like putting on safety gear is taking too long. Don't let this bother you.

My father and grandfather both worked in construction and they have both lost a significant amount of hearing. Sometimes I feel like I am screaming at them just so they can hear me. Both swear it was from construction equipment and power tools. To keep this from happening to me I decided I would wear hearing protection. Construction workers weren't really wearing hearing protection in those days. I would often be the only guy on a huge jobsite wearing ear plugs. Some of the comments that were made were absurd. My all-time favorite was... "you must have girly ears, that's why your putting tampons in them". If you do not have resolve in what you are doing, people will talk you out of doing it. 25

years later I have better hearing than most guys my age who are in the construction field. I've even had guys tell me they wish they would've been smart enough to wear ear plugs like I did. In short, don't worry about other people. Do whatever will ensure you live a longer and better life. Be safe.

NUMBER 8

Walk with Purpose

Walk with purpose? This may seem like an odd one but I can't tell you how many times a boss has mentioned how he liked how this guy or that guy walked quickly everywhere he went. I thought about this a lot. If two guys did the same task, like running out to their truck to grab a tool, but one guy walked quickly and the other moseyed about, who do you think would be perceived as the more productive employee?

There was an older guy I used to work with who was a slow walker. He had years of knowledge and was an excellent carpenter when it came to knowing how to do things. However, he moseyed around when he did things. He slowly strolled out to the porta john, slowly brought in his tools, and slowly carried materials etc. He was nicknamed "Droopy Dog". He was laid off every winter before people with a ¼ of his abilities because he was perceived as "lazy" or "slow".

I'll share another story. I got a job once with a company installing seating in a baseball stadium. To install these things, you have to assemble what feels like a million pieces. I got paired with a guy who had worked at this company for around 20 years. He was confident in his abilities and knew the parts inside and out. He decided he would layout the parts that were less numerous and much lighter in weight. I can't really blame him; I probably would've done the same thing. The mistake he made though was that he did this at an "old man's pace". He was not an old man. Being the new guy (and a little nervous), I decided I would grab as many parts as I could and walk as fast as I could to lay everything out. I laid out 4 to 5 times the amount that the other guy did. This was a big job for this company and the "big wigs" were always showing up unannounced and secretly watching us from the press boxes. I kept this up for days and was even told, by the guy I was paired with, to slow down. He said, "you're making me look bad". Because I was new (and still a little nervous) I did not slow down. Several days later our main boss pulled me aside. He admitted he had been watching me work for days without me knowing it and that he appreciated my pace. He promised I would still have a job even after this big project was over. He kept his word and I worked for that company for over 10 years.

Perception is paramount. You may not know as much as the next guy, but if you're walking with purpose and appearing to be "on a mission", your employer will perceive you as equal or greater in value to your fellow coworkers.

NUMBER 9

Keep your Work Area Clean

Maintaining a clean work area is as important to doing a good job as is using the correct tools. Construction can get messy, especially during demolition, but that doesn't mean you have to work in a huge mess. As you work, stop occasionally to clean up. This sounds simple and it is, but it will make a world of difference on the work you are putting out. Also, this is a much safer way to work. If you are trying to carry materials and you are constantly tripping over things, you are asking for an injury to happen. When a work area starts to get messy, you can feel the stress start to build. You get frustrated easier; you rush and mistakes happen. I know at times it will feel like you do not have time to stop and clean up for a second but it will save you time in the long run. Also, if your boss or the client shows up, it will appear that you are more professional and skilled for the work at hand. Clients are eager to monitor progress and show others how construction is coming along. You want them to be able to walk around safely and feel good about the people they have hired. Perception is everything. Clean up! You will put out better work and you and your crew will be perceived as more professional.

NUMBER 10

Stay Busy

When I first started in construction, I wasn't always sure what I should be doing. I would get assigned a task, complete it, then awkwardly figure out what I needed to do next. Sometimes this was easy, someone would ask for my help and then I would go right into my next task. Sometimes though, it wasn't so easy. Maybe my boss ran out to get materials or I was just clueless on the next step. I would often hear the guys say, "if you're leaning, you're cleaning". Basically, the idea behind the phrase was "stay busy". If you run out of things to do and you find yourself standing around, pick up a broom and start cleaning up. When your boss or whoever comes back and is able to instruct you, they find you working and helping the project move forward not sitting around doing nothing. This will make a huge impression. You will appear to be a good worker, eager to learn and grow. The guys standing around get hollered at. Trust me, not only have I witnessed this first hand but I've hollered at guys myself just standing there doing nothing. There is ALWAYS something that can be done. Clean up the gang box, the tool shed, sweep the floor, pick up the spilled box of screws, whatever, just do something productive. I used to work with this foreman who was a beat down old man approaching 70 years old. We called him old man Charlie. Construction had taken a toll on this guy; he could barely walk! He was the first guy to jump up and grab a broom while waiting on the delivery truck or he would organize our materials when lunch was over and the rest of the crew was still sitting around chatting. Management and the crew loved this guy! How could you not? He led by example and although he was old and beat down, his jobs ran smoothly and on time. Be old man Charlie and stay busy!

NUMBER 11

Measure Twice, Cut Once

We've all heard this one before. I almost didn't include it because well, we've all heard it before. However, stop and actually think about this one. It is easier and faster to check and re-check a measurement than to inaccurately cut a piece of wood or material. If you cut it too short the board is ruined and you can no longer use it. Maybe it can be used again somewhere else, but you will almost always waste time and also material. If you cut it too long, you will waste time having to then go back and cut it again. This old proverb has made its' way into the teachings of many business programs. It's more than a literal saying. It also means that anything worth doing is worth doing correctly and accurately, so double checking a decision before taking action will only ensure that the best decision is made. I've measured things countless times then been stopped on my way to the saw to talk about another aspect of the project. On my way back to the saw I realize I now can't remember if it was "something and 5/8 or something and 5/16". If I decide to go with what I thought it was instead of measuring again, I can bet that my guess will be wrong. That's carpentry, it's the law of nature or something. That is why measure twice, cut once has become such a famous saying in construction and many other businesses. If you haven't heard it yet, you will. Do it.

NUMBER 12

Stay Off your Phone

Cell phones and in particular, smart phones have no doubt made the world better in a lot of ways, but they also have their downside. Tech addiction is a real problem and I have seen guys first hand get on their phone every chance they get. This is an extremely quick way to be seen as a problem employee. Construction, for better or worse, is still run by "old School" guys. I still to this day work with guys who don't own a computer, have email, and can't even turn on a laptop! My company tries to implement computer trainings on a regular basis for a variety of reasons from safety to learning skills and there are always guys who need to be brought into the office to be walked through the process. These guys working next to the "smartphone generation" creates friction all the time. I constantly get calls from guys complaining about people spending too much time on their phone. I always respond by telling them to make it known to that employee that they are on their phone too much and if they can't stop to look for employment elsewhere. Phones create a reduction in productivity, create liability for drivers, and can be a safety issue for employees. A lot of companies are now implementing cell phone policies where you can only use them at scheduled times. People have families and may need them available and that's ok, but if you can, leave the phone in the truck.

NUMBER 13

Take Pride in your Work

I don't care what you are working on, take pride in your work. If you are sweeping the floor, do a good job, move things, sweep all of the floor not just part of it. You should approach every task with a sense of pride. Pretend that everything you are doing will be judged intensely by your boss, mother, father, or President of the United States. If you wouldn't want someone to see what you've done, you haven't done a good enough job. This is a simple concept but one that needs mentioned. Too many carpenters do things with the attitude that "no one will notice" or "that's good enough". It's not. Take the time to do it right and you will never have worry about what people are thinking about your work. Over the years I've witnessed plenty of carpenters who weren't the fastest, but were always on the "favorite list" because when it came down to it, you could always count on them to do a great job. You could send these carpenters to do anything. You could send them to do special projects at a new client's home, fix someone else's shoddy work, or trust them to work on the part of the job that will be on display for everyone to see. By taking pride in their work, they made themselves valuable. Valuable employees get promoted and if you want to make a career in construction, you want to be promoted.

I like to judge my work by asking myself, "would I want this in my house?" If the answer is no, I make it right. If I have to undo it, I do. Everything I've ever done half-heartedly or incorrectly still haunts me to this day, so I just make it a habit to take pride in my work. I feel good about it and I know over the years my superiors have taken notice.

NUMBER 14

Don't be Afraid to Make Mistakes

To be a good carpenter you will ultimately need to make mistakes, a lot of them. This is par for the course. I know a lot of carpenters who were always afraid to try things because they were so terrified of failing. In the end, these were not good carpenters because they didn't know how to do very much. I'm not suggesting you gamble with expensive material and put your job or the reputation of your employer on the line, just that you will need to be ok with failure.

I remember once when I was a young apprentice and my neighbor asked if I was able to replace his front door with a new one that he bought at Home Depot. I had never done this before but I wanted the opportunity to try so I said "yeah, I do it all the time". Now it depends on how you look at this whether it was a good idea or not. First, I agreed to do it for $100. It took me 14 hours on a Saturday to finally complete. That's a measly $7.15 an hour, but I had to buy some additional trim pieces that I messed up which brought my hourly wage to about $5 an hour. I could tell he was losing faith in my abilities as the hours ticked by and I made countless mistakes along the way. In the end though, he had a beautiful new front door that really helped transform the look of his home. Was it worth my time and aggravation? Absolutely! I learned so much from that one Saturday making mistake after mistake. I LEARNED from the mistakes and as long as you are learning from them, mistakes are your friends.

NUMBER 15

Don't Put your Hands in your Pockets

I know you're probably thinking, "why can't I put my hands in my pocket?". I've thought about why this is and I have some theories, but I can tell you, construction people hate when you put your hands in your pockets. The main reason is that it appears you are lazy. If your hands are in your pockets you are not doing work. You can't, your main tool to do work is shoved down in your pockets. It can also appear disrespectful. Disrespectful? Yeah, I know, but I looked it up on the internet and there is this famous (infamous) photograph of a famous Rugby player whose grand slam winning team was meeting Queen Elizabeth II. He's standing there with his hands in his pocket, and I have to admit, he looks disrespectful. Was he really being disrespectful? I doubt it. He would later go on to say his hands were sweaty and he was trying to dry them off before she got to him, but the damage had been done. He was torn apart on social media and he will forever be known as "disrespectful hands in pockets guy".

Experts have analyzed this and there are all sorts of psychological reasons they say you should not put your hands in your pocket. Everything from looking dishonest, to looking timid. This faux pas extends outside of the construction industry and apparently is a big deal in the military as well. I can personally attest to the construction industry though. I was scared to get things out of my pocket for a while in the beginning of my career for fear someone would scream at me. Just remember, you can't climb the ladder of success with your hands in your pocket.

NUMBER 16

Learn Construction Lingo

If you are new to construction, you will quickly realize there are a ton of words and phrases you will need to learn. I remember thinking to myself on many occasions, "what is this guy even talking about?". You will also realize at some point that guys call the same things, different things, which makes it even more challenging. Pay attention and you should be able to pick it up quickly.

One good rule of thumb to help in the beginning is that often, a tool will be called by the tool company name instead of what it is actually called. For example, many trades use tongue-and-groove pliers or slip-joint pliers, but when someone asks you to grab those for them, they will ask you to get them a pair of Channellocks. This can be confusing because like in the example, Channellock makes a huge assortment of tools, but only one is commonly called channellocks. This happens because a new tool will be manufactured and popularized by only one company and the tradesmen may not really know what the official name is. On the side of the tool the company will print their name and just like that, the tool is known as channellocks (or another tool company name).

Another thing that makes this more challenging is that guys will frequently call things the wrong name. I remember when I got sent to the store to buy a 50lb box of pan heads (screws) and when I made it back to the jobsite everyone was upset with me. Did I buy the wrong screws? No, I bought pan heads, but they were really wanting wafer head screws, but pan heads are what everyone called them. Learn everything you can, pay attention and if you get sent to the store to buy pan heads, take a couple with you to show the store clerk.

NUMBER 17

Learn the Tape Measure Inside and Out

As a carpenter you will use a tape measure ALL day long. Learn how to use it inside and out. Make sure you can not only read it but read it quickly. Look up online tests and see if a friend or family member will time you. There is nothing more frustrating than working with someone who takes a long time to read a tape. Again, construction is generally always time sensitive and "old timers" will have no patience for people who can't read a tape quickly.

I was on a job years ago and a new apprentice showed up. He claimed he knew what he was doing and that he's been in construction for years (side note: So many new guys who have no idea what they are doing will claim they have years of experience. When it comes out that they don't, it just makes people more frustrated with them.). The guys then had him read off measurements for cutting ceiling tile. He started calling out 20 inches and 3 of those little lines, 14 inches and 6 of those little lines. The guys thought it was hilarious for a couple of minutes until it was uncovered that this was indeed how he read a tape measure. They ate this poor kid alive (figuratively speaking of course). They dogged him so bad he did not show up after the first day. If you are not versed in reading a tape, practice and be honest about your abilities.

You will also want to spend some time picking a tape measure that works well for you. There are different styles and types. As a piece of advice, I would

NOT get one with the fractions listed. You will rely on them and when you are forced to use one with only the lines you will struggle. Force yourself to learn a regular old tape right from the beginning. You will thank me later.

NUMBER 18

Try to Anticipate what Comes Next

Construction is like anything else and has a "flow" to it. You want to be a worker who flows with your team. To do this, learn to anticipate what comes next in the order of operations. A lot of guys, especially new guys, will ask you what to do, do it, then stand there until they are told what to do next. This slows down the flow. Have you ever watched guys work together and think to yourself, man these guys work well together? Part of the reason is the synergy created from working with each other over the years, but the main reason is they learned what the other one needs next and starts the process before he or she gets to it.

Let's say you're hanging drywall with another worker and they are screwing off the last sheet. Don't just stand there and wait. Get the next sheet brought over, cut it to the height the last 12 sheets were, mark out the studs, cut the outlet out etc. Have it ready so when they are done, you can throw up the next sheet and keep moving. If you are constantly waiting for the other person to be the lead, you are interrupting the flow. Learning what comes next will take time, but once you do, you will become a valuable asset to your team.

NUMBER 19

Research at Home

Show up to work having done a little research. Let's say that you know you will be installing a drop ceiling in the morning. Maybe you've never done this before. Your boss is probably aware of this, but why not learn what you can before you start. At home that night, look it up on the computer. Youtube is your friend. There are countless how-to videos on almost every subject you can think of. There are many on the very example above. I know this because one day I was trying to explain drop ceilings to someone and was amazed to find numerous videos that did a great job explaining every aspect of installing drop ceilings.

Even if you still feel clueless after reading about a topic and watching videos, you are so much further along than you were when you started. Small things like this get noticed even if it doesn't feel like it. You will also be more confident during the learning process which will allow you to absorb the material better. Self-education is one of the fastest routes to rising above the competition. If you are reading this book, you are already someone who wants to learn as much as you can. Turn this into one of your many strengths.

NUMBER 20

Be Patient

"Patience and perseverance have a magical effect before which difficulties disappear and obstacles vanish." – John Quincy Adams

Patience is a skill that can be used in all areas of your life, but it is extremely helpful to you in construction. Things will not, I repeat, will NOT go as you had planned on a construction site. There will be overly optimistic/delusional people who say if you plan accordingly that jobs should run smoothly. Don't trust them! It will not run smooth. I'm being a little dramatic but also very truthful. If I had been impatient over my career, I'm not sure I would've enjoyed it very much. The stress may have killed me.

You will without a doubt start a project one day where you allotted a certain amount of time to complete. That time will come and go and you will still have plenty to do. This is where bosses and employees start to go awry. You must now practice your new found construction patience and stay the course. Otherwise, the job will suffer and so will your attitude. I encourage you to remember these occurrences. As you grow into a leader on the job and beyond, your tendency might be to get frustrated with your crew for taking too long to complete a job. You may even think they are "goofing" off (and maybe they are), but be patient and learn what you can about the situation. Learn how you can best help facilitate the results you seek. Patience can sometimes be extremely hard to conjure up in the moment, but the implementation will be worth it.

NUMBER 21

Master the Framing Square

The framing square, also known as the steel square or the carpenter's square is one of the most underappreciated tools carpenters have in their arsenal. Some argue this is the most useful tool used by a carpenter. Understanding the square will allow you to measure in 10ths to 100ths of an inch, determine board feet, figure bracing for post and beam construction, change measurements into fractions, convert a square beam to an eight-sided post, and figure the rise and run of a complicated staircase. Before the square was invented, you would've needed to be highly skilled in math principles to figure this stuff out. Once the tables on the square are learned, a new world of knowledge can be unlocked. By mastering the scales and tables an apprentice has started his move into the master craftsman category. Just a few hours each week of quiet study on the topic of the square can give you the confidence and skills required to rise above your fellow craftsman. I know this may seem like strange advice to some, but every craftsman I have ever met who could use the square with ease, left me in awe and in a cloud of envy.

NUMBER 22

Choose what You are Good at

This might sound like a strange bit of advice, but there will come a time when this will make sense. I do think that everyone should try to learn as many carpentry skills as humanly possible, but carpentry encompasses so many different skills. You will definitely prefer doing some things over others. Carpenters frame buildings, pour concrete, work on highways, install drywall, mud drywall, lay floors, install trim, fabricate millwork, etcetera. You will likely not love every task. I know I didn't. That being said, why not focus on the aspects of carpentry that you do love?

As you start your career in construction, the industry, the economy, timing or whatever forces currently in play, will push you down a certain path. The path you are pushed down might not exactly be the one you want. The carpenters that work on highways are a great example. Do you really want to be standing on the side of a busy freeway with cars buzzing by you at 70 mph in 20-degree weather? You might get rained out and have to go home upon just arriving. Work slows down worse than other sections of construction in the winter. However, the pay is higher due to these factors. I personally think this sounds miserable. However, there are guys who love the road crew and maybe you're one of them. That's awesome! Those should be the guys that are out there. I chose to focus on finish carpentry because I enjoyed that more and I also enjoyed the fact that I could work inside year-round. Most finish carpentry needs to be in a climate-controlled building, so you will not need to work in the rain or in freezing conditions. The downside is that when it is beautiful outside, you are stuck inside and unable to enjoy the amazing weather. Each specialty comes with its own set of advantages and disadvantages.

Let's say you got hired on at a concrete company as your first construction job. You work there for a year or a season and then get laid off. Look for new work, don't wait for them to call you back. Try an interior systems company (drywall, etc.) or a finish carpentry company, or whoever might be hiring. Work that job for a while and compare it to the other(s). You will quickly realize which one is best suited for you. If you stick around too long in a specialty that you don't love, it will become harder to find jobs in the areas that you do love. Put this advice in the back of your head because you will notice if you start to get stuck doing only one thing. We are all better off if construction workers are doing the jobs they want to be doing.

NUMBER 23

Ask Advice (Especially from the Old-Timers)

Do not be afraid to ask your fellow co-workers for advice. You will quickly find out that some people will LOVE to give advice and others will basically shrug you off. Don't let the people who shrug you off discourage you from asking. I remember asking one of my coworkers once if he would help me scribe a countertop to the wall when I was an apprentice. He literally said to me that he gets no benefit from helping me become a better carpenter. He said if I learn what he knows then I could possibly take his position in the company. Wow! I couldn't believe it. I thought about it later though and I realized he probably didn't know very much if he was worried about teaching a newbie one small skill. I asked another coworker and he was more than happy to show me the way.

I've found that the old-timers are full of tips and tricks that make many of the tasks easier. Many enjoy taking a young apprentice "under their wing" and passing on what they have learned. If one of these old-timers takes a liking to you, take advantage and pay attention! You will learn invaluable information that you can't get anywhere else, not in any text books or even in any college courses.

I was lucky enough to work with a guy called "Old Man Obert". He always asked the boss to work with me and gave me countless advice. The things he taught me I've used throughout my entire career. I appreciated everything he did for me and I made it a point to pay it forward whenever I could. Little things can make a huge difference for someone learning the craft. I hope this book is another way that I can help.

NUMBER 24

Finish One Task at a Time

Always finish a task before moving on to the next one. Your boss can't stand over your shoulder and check everything you are doing as you are doing it, nor would you want them to. Being able to complete the tasks you are given is key to being perceived as someone who can get the job done. You want to be someone who can get the job done or you will guarantee your spot at the top of the layoff list. The boss has a ton of things to do and worry about. He may only be able to show up, give orders for the day/week, and then head out. He is depending on his crew to get everything done.

Let's say your job was to go back through and finish screwing off the 100 sheets of drywall the crew hung that week. You start and only get part of the way through and then start working on another task. A few days later the drywall finishers show up and start mudding the walls and they discover that they are not all ready. First of all, drywall finishers are historically the grumpiest fellows on a jobsite (I've never figured out why) and they will "rip you a new one". Also, they will complain to the boss and you will be the guy they can't trust to complete tasks. Reputations can be extremely difficult to shake, especially bad ones, so always finish your tasks.

NUMBER 25

Learn How to Add/Subtract Fractions (in your Head)

As a carpenter you will use fractions every single day. Whatever the reason, America never switched to the metric system and I do not envision them doing so. I remember some talk in my younger years of America making the switch but that talk has all but died since. That means we are on the standard system for the foreseeable future. For better or worse we are a country made of fractions.

The good news is that most tape measures only go to 1/16 of an inch. There will be no need to know off the top of your head say 198/362" because it will be written 9/16". You will need to know though how to add or subtract 9/16" +/– 3/8" or other similar fractions that go from halves to sixteenths. At first this will seem difficult and there will undoubtedly be some angry journeyman waiting on you to give him a dimension which requires the addition or subtraction of fractions while you awkwardly do the math in your head, but you will pick it up. The faster that you do, the better off you will be.

When I was a young (and strikingly handsome) apprentice, I had an instructor who would give us timed pop-up quizzes on fractions. Later, maybe the same day or same week or even weeks apart, he would pull out the same quiz and time us again. I found this immensely helpful. I am competitive by nature and I can't stand getting bad grades even if they didn't technically count as traditional "grades". I studied on my own time and found ways to work with fractions more quickly. Before long I was getting all the answers correct and before the time ran out. If you are motivated, grab some tests online and practice, practice, practice.

NUMBER 26

Don't Waste a Trip

I used to hear this advice all the time. This is an easy one to follow and it will definitely make a good impression on your boss. Let's say you are working and you have to use the facilities (sadly, most of the time it's a porta-potty), grab as much trash you can carry and take it out to the dumpster on your way out. Maybe you're walking back into the building from lunch and your boss is parked out front with a truck full of materials to bring in. Stop and grab some things and bring them in on your way in. That's it! That's all you need to do to help solidify a good impression. You're already going that way, only you're not going empty handed. You will look busy even when you were really on your way to a break.

      This even helped me once when it technically shouldn't have. It was a Friday and we had worked hard all week. We only get a 30-minute lunch which some days is just too short. We decided we would take matters into our own hands and leave early for lunch to go to Bob Evans. As you probably realize, 30 minutes isn't enough time to sit down and eat at Bob Evans. I grabbed a bunch of trash to take out to the dumpster on my way to my truck. As I was throwing the trash in the dumpster our boss rolled up to check-in on us. I was "caught" working which made me look good and I ran to the porta-john and texted everybody to turn around and go back to work. When our boss walked in, everybody was working instead of heading to Bob Evans. Crisis averted and I was the hero for the day. Not exactly my proudest moment, but an example of how going the extra mile can help you succeed. I wasn't sure if I should put this story in the book (again, not my proudest moment), but I decided to keep it in after much debate. I think real life stories help illustrate the bigger picture.

NUMBER 27

Slow is Smooth, Smooth is Fast

This is an old Navy SEAL saying. It is also a worthwhile nugget of wisdom that can be applied to many industries, including; you guessed it, construction. No matter what the task is that you are performing, perform it slowly. This allows your brain to ingrain the correct motor skills and thought into the process. If you rush, and I can attest to this, you will fumble through, thus slowing you down and making the task take longer had you slowed down and done everything the proper way and in the proper order.

I used to work for a construction company that specialized in installing cabinets and millwork. I often worked with a guy who worked there for over 20 years. Nothing about him appeared to be "fast". He spoke slowly and appeared to be thinking heavily before he responded to questions. This guy dominated everyone in regard to how many cabinets he would install. I would ask him how he was so fast and he would always say that he just took his time. That never made any sense to me. I would watch him work on occasion and he never seemed to be moving very fast only methodically. When I came across the adage "slow is smooth, smooth is fast", this guy immediately came to mind.

In the end, slowing down while working on a task will improve overall efficiency and performance. This may seem like it's going against some of my earlier advice (i.e. walk with purpose) but, those are things that require little to no thought. The actual work should be approached separately, perception vs. reality are different things. Think bigger picture in your life and take note of who gets things done. It just might be the guy who "appears" to work slow.

NUMBER 28

Be Thick Skinned

According to the Cambridge Dictionary, the term thick-skinned means; not easily hurt by criticism. That is a simple definition in regard to construction. In construction it means; the ability to not be hurt by criticism...*on steroids*! People will be overly harsh. You need to know this going in because for a lot of newbies, this is a huge shock. Some people may have gone through life and never had anyone "rip them a new one". I promise you though, it will happen. This is not one of construction's best features. It is however, the reality.

As I mentioned earlier, construction is usually on a tight schedule. As the days pass and the work commences, someone is surely starting to feel the pressure. A little mistake can feel like a huge disaster to a foreman or boss trying to meet deadlines. Here you are, trying to do your best (at least I presume) and let's say you laid out walls 6" off from where they need to be. When this is uncovered this could set off your boss or even a fellow carpenter. It's not the end of the world but it may feel like that after the harsh words you may receive. You may get told you're an idiot or asked why you're too stupid to read prints. You may get put on floor sweeping duties or told to do something any dummy could figure out. Just apologize and do your best to remedy the problem. If you're told to do something else just do that and learn from your mistake. If you have to go back at lunch or after work and read prints etc. to figure out what you did wrong, you should. Also, be prepared for the guys to bring up whatever mistake you made RELENTLESSLY.

I'm not saying that the way things go down in construction are just, but I do want you to be prepared for it. All you can do is learn from your mistake and do your best to not let it happen again. Some guys have a tendency to argue back and point fingers at others. This will not help. I've seen people get fired from the yelling and nasty words exchanged after a small mistake that was like 15 minutes to fix. I've seen fist fights break out as well and then usually both people get fired. Getting angry and retaliating is not worth it! Then there are guys who get all bent out of shape and look like they are on the verge of tears. This will not help either and if the guys see that you may be sensitive, they will pour on the torment times

1,000! I've witnessed torment so bad that guys have quit in tears.

The suggestion that you need to develop a thick-skin is not a pretty characteristic of construction. There's a lot of research about how developing thick-skin could actually be hurting us. This is a little too deep for a book like this and I'm not asking you to change who you are. I just want you to be prepared. There can be a lot of stress in the workplace (especially in construction) and people will not always handle it appropriately. If you know this coming in, you won't flip out when someone decides to come at you unprofessionally.

NUMBER 29

Always Act Professionally

People will come at you unprofessionally (see number 28). They may even be downright inappropriate. If you're like me, your first thought might be to fight fire with fire. Avoid this trap. Always act professionally. When these unwelcomed situations arise, I like to pretend my mother is watching. This way I can handle the situation appropriately and be proud of how I handled myself later. This doesn't mean you have to be a pushover or subject yourself to abuse of any kind. Remain calm and address the situation in a manner that makes sense. I've told coworkers, bosses, and even owners that their behavior was unacceptable. I wasn't always beloved by all, but I know everyone respected me and how I handled myself.

I've broken up fights over what radio station to listen to, who unplugged the extension cord, it's not break time, someone taking someone else's hammer, etc. The list is embarrassingly long. Even if you can't do anything about it, let people know that their behavior won't be tolerated. Sometimes this will be enough. I've had people come to me later and apologize because they had calmed down and were embarrassed of how they acted. If you always act professionally you will be respected and never have to worry about what you've done later.

NUMBER 30

Make Friends with the Other Trades

This book focuses mainly on becoming a carpenter but this advice goes for everybody, no matter what trade you decide on. Make friends with the other tradespeople on the job. You will work beside electricians, plumbers, iron workers, HVAC techs, data installers, floor layers etc. Say good morning and hello. If someone asks you to move your truck or your material, do it without attitude even if it's irritating. Do favors, work together, and look out for each other. On some projects you may see these people for months or even years. You may even see them on your following projects. Building a rapport can benefit you on so many levels. First, you will be happier. Also, your job will be easier because the other trades will lend a hand.

I once received an entire semi-trailer of casework for a 2nd story that was supposed to be for a 1st floor offload. I had a couple options and none were very good, especially the one where my team and I were going to have to carry everything up the stairs. We usually rent a lull lift and boom them all up through an open window, but we had not rented one because we were not expecting a 2nd floor offload. I called the rental place and was told that all lifts were 2 weeks out! This was going to be a serious problem for scheduling and also our job progress. I remembered the electricians had a lull lift out back that they used on occasion. I had befriended the electricians and their boss by doing small favors and being kind as the job progressed. Instead of having them move their rough-ins to accommodate our cabinets, I would swap cabinets around our slide them around to make things work. Because the problems were their fault and not ours, they were tickled to work with me and have me solve the problems without any additional work on their end. I asked their boss if I could borrow their lift for the day and was delighted when he replied with, "absolutely"! Not only did he allow us to borrow it, but he supplied a worker to run it for us the entire time! This was a lifesaver and allowed us to proceed on schedule. It also saved us a ton of money. Lift rentals for even one day can approach close to $1,000 by the time you pay for delivery, fuel and pick-up.

This was all able to happen because I had fostered a friendly and harmonious relationship with the electricians. I have been on jobs where even if the other trades were in a position to help, they refused. I've witnessed other trades break off plumbers' stub-outs in walls, cut electricians wires, mar up painted walls, damage cabinets and all sorts of terrible things. It doesn't have to be like this and it is easier and more enjoyable to go the way of togetherness. Like the old adage says, you catch more flies with honey than you do vinegar.

NUMBER 31

Work Overtime

Depending on who you are, this is either a blessing or a curse. If you don't mind working longer hours or working weekends and making additional money, construction is the industry for you. I have mentioned several times in this book that construction rarely goes according to plan, but that doesn't mean deadlines can change as well. Sometimes deadlines can move and other times companies need guys to work extra hours to get back on schedule. In my experience, overtime will happen on almost every project. Sometimes just at the end of the project and sometimes it starts as soon as you show up. It all depends on the need of the project.

In the beginning of my career, I loved overtime. I volunteered every single time. I was a single guy living on my own trying to make ends meet and the extra cash really helped. As I got older, more established and started a family, overtime became a little less appealing. I got to a point where I just wanted to be home with my family. Some guys were the opposite and wanted to work very little in the beginning of their career but now that they have a family need all the extra cash they can get. I can tell you it's a lot easier to work all that overtime when you're young and have less responsibilities.

No matter what my preference was, when the project needed it, I always tried to help out. Your boss will appreciate it if you are someone who goes the extra mile and pitches in extra hours when the project needs it. As you develop and grow in your career you can better navigate the number of hours you will need to work. Getting started my advice would be to work the overtime when you are asked. It won't go unnoticed.

NUMBER 32

Always Build Plumb, Square, and Level

If for you are unsure of the definition of plumb, square or level, your first step is to make sure you understand what those terms mean. I was shocked to learn a guy I had worked with for a couple of years did not understand the term plumb. Although he was embarrassed, he insisted he always "leveled vertically", which is how he phrased it. I had to take his word for it, but I did always wonder what he set about doing when someone told him to make sure it was plumb. He was probably too afraid to ask for fear of ridicule until that day we worked together. I'm glad he finally asked.

I will go over these briefly, but I want to reiterate that if you are unsure what these terms mean, please read about them. Plumb means to be true or perfectly straight in a vertical plane. The best way to check if something is plumb is with a plumb-bob (perfect name), a level used vertically or one of today's fancy plumb lasers. Level is completely straight in the horizontal plane and can also be found using a level or a laser. To build square is to have perfect 90-degree corners (or right angles). You check this by using squares (see number 21) or by using the 3 4 5 method (see number 33). These definitions were oversimplified but in reality, they are pretty simple to follow and understand.

Now I know I just said to build plumb, square and level and you should always start there, but I should clarify a point before someone writes to tell me I'm wrong. There will be situations where you won't. This happens generally on old houses or renovation projects. Some buildings/houses were either built out of square or plumb or have settled over time. This creates a problem when you put something "true" up against it or beside it etc. The rule of thumb is to make it as visually appealing as possible even if that means leaving it out of plumb or level. This does not happen a lot but it will happen. I'll never forget spending hours installing window and door casing on a 1920's farmhouse just for my boss to walk in and say, "that looks like crap"! That was my first lesson in making sure things are visually appealing. The lessons that are easily remembered are the ones that were hardest to learn. Unfortunately, you will learn best by screwing up. As a general rule though, always start out with the intention of building plumb, square and level.

NUMBER 33

Learn the 3-4-5 Method

Carpentry doesn't always have rules written in stone for every situation and one man's method might not be the way the next guy does it.

As outlined in number 32 there are some guidelines to help you achieve your desired results. The 3-4-5 method can help you achieve building plumb, square and level. More accurately this method is used to assist you in building square.

Carpenters often use speed squares and framing squares to check layouts but when the layout is large enough these squares are simply too small to guarantee the accuracy needed. Large remodeling and construction projects such as laying out the foundation of a house or walls often employ the 3-4-5 triangle technique to ensure accurate 90-degree angles.

I found an article by the Concord Carpenter (check him out online) to help me explain. He says:

3-4-5 Rule Layman's Terms:

If the short side of the triangle is 3 feet, and the leg that extends from it 90 degrees is 4 feet, the hypotenuse, or longest leg, will be 5 feet.

This technique simply requires that the carpenter create a triangle in the corner of the lines that are to be square (90 degrees) to each other.

The 3-4-5 triangle must have

- *One side (triangle leg) that is 3 feet long*

- *A second side (triangle leg) that is 4 feet long*
- *A third side, connecting the two legs measuring 5 feet long*

Any triangle with sides of 3, 4 and 5 feet will have a 90-degree angle opposite the 5 foot side. The beauty and simplicity of this technique is if the carpenter or builder needs to increase accuracy on larger walls or structures, any multiple of the 3-4-5 rule can be deployed.

Examples of the 3-4-5 Rule

- 3-4-5
- 6-8-10
- 9-12-15
- 12- 16-20
- 15-20-25

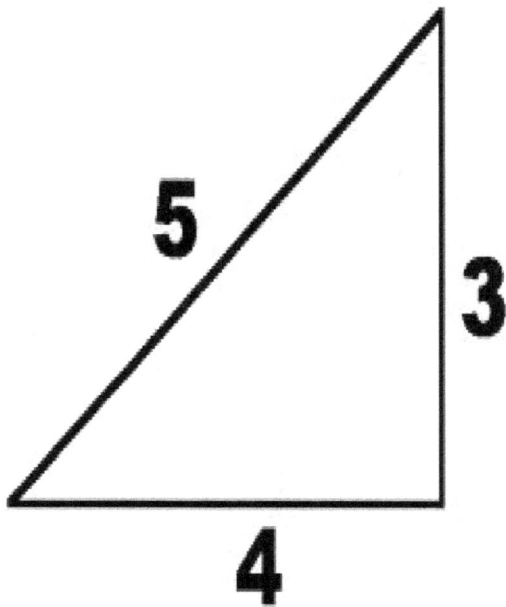

Why Dos This Work?

- *Mathematically why does the 3-4-5 method for squaring corners create a perfect right angle?*
- *In Geometry, a well-known method of constructing a right angle is to employ the Pythagorean Theorem. The mathematician, Pythagoras,*

discovered a relationship between the sides of any right triangle that is now known as the Pythagorean Theorem; he proved that the square of the longest side (the hypotenuse) is equal to the sum of the squares of the remaining two sides.

- This is written as the following equation:
- $a^2 + b^2 = c^2$
- A and B are the two legs of the right triangle and C is the hypotenuse. If we substitute the numbers from a 3-4-5 triangle into this formula, we then have: 9" + 16" = 25"

Remembering the 3-4-5

Using triangle dimensions of 3, 4 and 5 is easy to remember and deploy, there are no difficult equations to remember and the 3-4-5 method will always produce a perfect right angle very time.

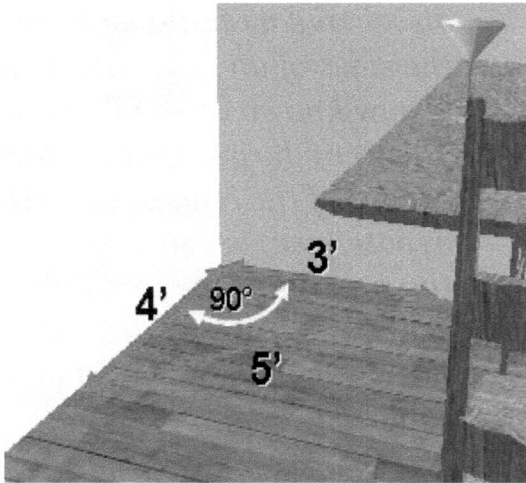

What If the Last Measurement is Off?

- When using the 3-4-5 method for squaring corners, if your last measurement [the third side] connecting the two legs measuring [5 foot side] is off and not square you will need to make adjustments.
- Adjustments usually mean moving the one side, either the 3-foot or 4-foot triangle leg in or

out to obtain the square 5-foot measurement.

I've found this trick to be helpful over the years and I think you will too. Remember, Google is your friend. When building, making a small mistake in the beginning can multiply itself as you go forward. Learning how to avoid those mistakes early puts you ahead of the pack.

NUMBER 34

Take Advantage of any Free Training Offered

I once worked for a company who installed telescoping bleachers as part of their niche. In order to install these, you had to be certified by the factory that manufactured them. I didn't necessarily love building bleachers, but I knew being trained would ultimately help me. I signed up and happily agreed to travel to a school out of town and take the course. It wasn't a very fun course, quite frankly, it kind of sucked, but I suffered through. This was right before the great recession that would go on to ravage the construction industry. I was later told that when the higher ups were deciding on who to keep and who to let go, my certification class firmly slid me onto the "keep" list.

I realize a lot of us got into construction because "school" wasn't our forte. If you're reading this book though, you have the propensity to self-educate. You are already leaps and bounds ahead of your future competition when it comes to getting ahead. That being said, if your employer or local high school offer some sort of free training or course on construction, take it! This can all go on a resume or be mentioned during an interview. If you plan on staying with a particular company and they see that you have taken every course they offer, you will show your enthusiasm and motivation to excel. You will become an asset worth cultivating and more importantly, worth keeping around. If a company has spent time and money training you and grooming you to be the type of employee they seek, they would be remiss by letting you take your talents elsewhere. That is business 101. So, do everything you can to make it hard for an employer to get rid of you. Education cannot be denied. Even if somebody did let you go, you will still have the knowledge and training behind you and this becomes part of your appeal for your next endeavor.

NUMBER 35

Minimize Waste

Taking time to properly plan your project will help minimize waste. One of the best mentors I've ever had used to say, "if you're cutting more than 2'-0" off a board, you're cutting the wrong board". This stuck with me throughout my whole career. When I would cut material and it was clearly wasteful, I could hear him in my head yelling at me. His advice makes sense. I know there will be situations that you won't have a choice, but it is a good rule to try to adhere to. Save your cutoffs and see if there are situations where you can use them elsewhere, for shims, blocking, or other applications. What doesn't get used goes right into the dumpster and is gone forever. This can not only hurt the bottom line of you or your employer, but it's also bad for the environment. Don't get rid of any material until you are certain it will be of no use.

If you are doing any kind of remodeling and you are ripping out things like bathroom vanities or light fixtures, save them. You can donate things like this to the Habitat for Humanity's Restore store. Donating these things can help you reach a desired LEED (Leadership in Energy and Environmental Design) score or qualify you for tax rebates. LEED is the most widely used green building rating system. Search online or more information. LEED information alone could be a book.

Take regular physical or mental notes on what material you need, constant trips to the hardware store will cost you time and money.

Planning is key. You might work your butt off and bring in jobs under hours but if you lose that profit to additional material and trips to the store, you're working harder and not making anybody more money.

NUMBER 36

Don't Touch Tools without Asking

Don't learn this tip the hard way. There are people who will become extremely agitated if you get into their toolbox without asking. Over time, you might work with the same people over and over and some will give you an open invite to get whatever you need out of their box. If they do not explicitly give you this invite, DON'T DO IT! I've seen people just almost fight over someone getting into their toolbox without asking. I personally never became angry, at least not on the first offense, but I understand why people don't want people just helping themselves to their tools. Tools are expensive, at least the good ones, and when you go to grab something and it's not there, you waste time looking for it and wondering if you have to go buy another one. Tools are how we make money. If a man thinks you are restricting his ability to make money, you are setting yourself up for inevitable conflict. Most carpenters will let you borrow whatever you need as long as you ask. They just want to make sure they know where it is so they can ensure they get it back. This is easy advice to follow, so make sure you do. You want to make allies in construction, not enemies. Always ask before you take.

NUMBER 37

Plot your Career Path

To get where you want to go, you have to figure how to get to get there. Formulating a plan will help you succeed in construction. You will be surprised how fast promotions can happen in construction, especially right now. If you have a plan, reaching your milestones will be easier and cleaner than just winging it. Let's say you want to become a safety manager. It would be smart to take any OSHA classes that you may have the opportunity to take. You might make your mission to get the top safety record in your company. Be proactive, volunteer to lead your crew's "toolbox talks" and if such a thing doesn't exist, start it. Maybe you want to be a project manager, take leadership classes that your company offers. If your company doesn't offer such classes, browse your local community college course listings. Many places offer certificates in just about any area of interest you may have. Opportunities exist, you just have to seek them out. I can tell you from experience that my career plateaued for several years until I sat down and figured out what I wanted to do, then took the necessary steps to make them happen.

NUMBER 38

Expand your Responsibilities

A surefire way to get noticed by the powers that be (your boss), is to go above and beyond. What do I mean by this? Well, all you have to do is do more than you are expected to do. Let's say you are told to pick up some of the trash around the jobsite. Most people would walk around and pick up the most offensive or large trash items and call it done. You, wanting to make an impression, should go around, pick ALL the trash up, sweep the floor and then organize the gang box or tool room. You also empty all the trash cans and reorganize any piles of material that have gotten sloppy from digging through them. This type of behavior will set you apart from the "clock punchers".

Here is another example. Most construction jobs start at 7:00 am. Try getting there at 6:30 am and unlocking the gang box. Start getting tools ready and extension cords strung out. The crew will show up and think to themselves that you are a superstar employee. A word of caution here; some people will try to discourage you from doing these kinds of things. They will feel threatened and call you a "suck up" and try to make fun of you. They want to continue to be lazy and they feel like you will make them look bad. You will have to learn to navigate this delicately and strategically, but in the end, you will be helping everyone out while at the same time helping yourself.

NUMBER 39

Be Innovative

The construction industry is constantly moving towards new technology. Some of the machines and tools currently in use are some of the most advanced technologies around. As you grow in your career you will continuously be a part of these new trends. Do not shy away from learning these new technologies. Seek opportunity. There is no doubt in my mind that some of these technologies will change our understanding of current building methods and spawn new job opportunities. Be willing to accept new innovations and keep your eyes open on new ways to use these new innovations for even broader use in the industry.

I have a great example in my personal business. We started using software (not necessarily intended for construction) for different service requests in our office. We had a guy who worked with the software every day and he started tweaking it little by little to automate and truly assist in our day to day operations. Eventually this thing grew into something so useful to our business that it became "our" software. We now lease the use of this software to other construction companies around our local area and even to some companies out of state. With the groundwork he laid, these other companies can make small tweaks to customize to their business and hit the ground running. All this was possible because he saw a need and then set about innovating a way to fill that need.

Now you might be saying to yourself, that's great but I'm not a computer genius. Don't worry, I'm not either. There are many ways in which someone can be innovative. You could come up with a tool cart that you can use on the jobsite that boosts your productivity. A process of installing (fill in the blank product). You could alter one of your current tools to be of better use. The possibilities are endless. We had a guy that worked for use that designed an adjustable jack for installing wall cabinets made from a car jack. He literally welds them in his garage and sells them to the other guys. I can remember when management went out to the jobsite and noticed all these cabinet jacks in use. Let me tell you, they were really impressed and that guy looked like a hero. You do not have to be Thomas Edison to come up with new innovations. Just keep your eyes open and constantly think about ways to make what you are doing easier and more efficient.

NUMBER 40

Be A Team Player

What do I mean when I say be a team player? Work well with others, that's a given, but I want you to dig deeper than that. You will almost always work with other people on projects, no matter what the project is. Look out for each other. Help each other succeed. Union workers literally call themselves brothers. I want you to think of others like that. Why? You will go further in your career and when it's all said and done, you can look back on your career and be proud of all you have accomplished.

As I stated before, construction is booming, but it might not always be like this. After the housing market collapsed and the subsequent recession hit around 2007, construction was not only *not* booming, people were struggling to find work. I can remember starting work with a new company around that time. The company culture there was cutthroat. The guys were so worried about keeping their job that they would "throw people under the bus" every chance they got. I remember having lunch with the guys one day and hearing stories of a couple projects that I screwed up that I had never set foot on. It was so bad that a couple guys had never even bothered to check if I had even worked on those jobs before they made up stories about me messing things up! I quickly got things cleared up and was able to illustrate how some people were "full of it". This era of my career was not my favorite but I can tell you this; the back stabbers were all eventually weeded out and the guys who tried to bring people up stuck around for many years. Some are still there today. Be a team player and avoid back-stabbing at all costs.

NUMBER 41

Master the Soft Skills

In construction, "hard skills" generally refer to the knowledge and abilities you would think you would need to perform your job. These refer to the ability to apply construction methods and techniques. There is a growing need for employees to develop "soft skills". These skills fall into the categories of personal attributes, interpersonal skills and problem-solving/decision-making skills. These are becoming increasingly more important as employers realize that employees who have real world skills and not just technical skills, help maintain a working environment that is safer and more efficient. There is a lot of research showing that these skills are as key to your success in construction as your technical abilities. Although this topic is vast and we could talk about it ad nauseam, this book is meant to make you aware of the basic skill set needed.

Some of the soft skills employers are looking for are:

- Emotional Intelligence
- Communication Skills (Written and Oral)
- Stress Management
- Professionalism
- Workplace Ethics
- Collaboration Skills (Team Work)
- Workplace Diversity Skills (Cultural Awareness)
- Social Intelligence
- Self-Management Skills

- Critical Thinking Skills (Problem -Solving)
- Negotiation
- Working Under Pressure
- Adaptability
- Resilience
- Influence
- Time Management
- Organizational Skills
- Trust Building
- Conflict Management
- Decision Making

This list may seem expansive and you are not required to "master" any or all of these, however improving on these traits will help you achieve higher success in the industry.

Unfortunately, there is no class or degree that will help you improve your soft skills. Improving is something you will have to make a conscious effort to improve. You will first have to gain self-awareness of your strengths and learn where you need to improve. From there you can develop your blind spots. This can be easier said than done. I recommend enlisting the help of your friends, family, colleagues and even former employers. You might ask them what soft skills come to mind when they think of you. If they have specific examples, that is even better. You may even discover things about yourself you didn't know before. Get feedback and do research online. There is a lot of helpful information on this topic.

NUMBER 42

Know the Rules

Wherever you decide to embark on your construction journey, you should try to familiarize yourself with some local rules or codes to save yourself some headache down the road. This is especially important if you get into commercial construction. Public spaces generally require builders to follow more stringent codes to ensure public safety. Building inspectors will undoubtedly become a regular feature on any construction site and it is there job to make sure things are done properly. Although a lot of contractors consider inspectors unnecessary or even cumbersome, the codes are there to keep occupants in buildings as safe as possible. There are some contractors who try to ignore building codes or do things without proper permits but this will usually end poorly. This can even set you on a path to getting sued.

The best route is to familiarize yourself with as many rules and guidelines as possible so you can build properly from the beginning. When I was an apprentice, I worked for a guy who remodeled office spaces. I was working on a new office space for a law firm that my boss chose to not get any inspections for. We were probably ¾ of the way complete when an inspector walked in. He was not happy and we had to "deconstruct" huge portions of the work we had completed. I don't know the details or the numbers but I can imagine that the project lost a ton of money. That company is no longer in business.

Knowing the rules and doing things correctly from the beginning will help you in the long run. The ability to stop and let your boss know that the prints are requiring you install something against code will add immense value to your employability.

NUMBER 43

Be a Leader

Be a leader. This one attribute will increase your promotability tenfold. If you showcase this skill on a regular basis, your employer will feel good about eventually putting you in charge of the team. Being a leader does not mean being bossy or barking orders. All you really have to do is work as if you owned the company and be a catalyst for keeping the project going.

I have a quick story that will help illustrate my point. I had just been hired at a new construction company and had worked there maybe a month or so. I was pulled off the job I was on to help out for the morning on another project. Our task was to uncrate these giant metal cabinets and carry them up the stairs and into their rooms. When I got there everyone was just standing around waiting on the foreman who had not shown up yet. After about 15 minutes the foreman called one of the guys and said he would not be there for another hour. Everyone just continued to stand around. I decided to go out to my truck and get some tools to start uncrating the cabinets. The other guys stood around chatting and watching me do all of this. I finished uncrating them and even took out all the trash. I wheeled the first one to the bottom of the stairs and said to the guys, "c'mon, at least help me carry them up". They did and we were half way done when the foreman arrived. We finished up and as I was driving back to the project I was originally working on, my boss called. Apparently, he had been on the job watching us from the mezzanine level. He said he saw me working by myself and being a leader. He thanked me for taking the initiative and promised me I would be a foreman soon. I was running work for them 3 weeks later. You never know who might be watching. Be a leader.

NUMBER 44

Keep an Updated Resume

Writing a resume can be tedious. Most people don't even know where to begin. A lot of us got into construction in the first place because we weren't brilliant writers and didn't know how we were going to go to college (me included). In today's world, you need a quality resume if you want to get increasingly better job positions. Your resume needs to be relevant, up to date, and tailored to the position in which you are applying. I recommend you work on your resume right away and then maintain it as you progress through your career. You don't want to wait until a possible opportunity appears and then hastily put one together the night before. A good resume will need to have a lot of information condensed into a smaller presentation. You will want to share it with your friends, family, and colleagues and then meticulously edit and proofread.

Remember, unless you are applying for a job within the company you are already employed, this is the first impression you will give to your new possible employer. Include any industry credentials, accomplishments, education, and previous work history. It may even be worth it to hire a professional resume writer to look over your resume and help steer you down the right path. Think about it, is $50 to $100 worth paying to help you land a job that pays you $20,000 more a year? Be creative and honest with your resume. Do your best to keep it up to speed and maintained. You will be miles ahead of the competition.

NUMBER 45

Be Willing to Travel

This will be easier for some than others. At this point in my career traveling is off limits. I have a wife and four kids at home and it's just too hard on everybody for me to be gone. That being said, in the beginning I traveled all the time. There were months when I traveled every week. Being able to go wherever you are needed improves your value. If you are early in your career and you are yet to start a family, willingness to travel should be something you add to your resume. There are still small companies that only operate locally, but they are becoming a thing of the past.

Remember, travel might be from one large city in your state to another large city in your state, not necessarily across country. The farther you have to go the less profit is available for your company because they have to pay your time and expense. Make yourself available for this, if your life changes and you can no longer travel, just be open and honest with your employer. When my family started to grow and traveling became a huge burden on my life, I sat down with my boss and explained this. He was happy to accommodate me so I could stay with the company. I had worked hard and became someone they did not want to lose.

NUMBER 46

Communicate your Career Goals

Sharing your career goals with your supervisor may seem like a scary proposition, but if done correctly, it can strengthen your relationship with your boss and open up better opportunities for your future. You will want to approach this as strategically as possible. Ideally, you've worked with your employer awhile and have a little insight on who your boss is as a person. Base your plan on past dealings and note what seemed to work or not work during communications. He or she ultimately holds the keys to your advancement and checking in regularly will at least keep you in the conversation in their mind. You will show sincere interest and they will know before recommending you that advancement is something you desire and will work for. Through conversations etc. you will also gain an understanding of what opportunities might be coming up. Knowing where you want to go and being able to communicate those goals will help you on your path to advancement.

NUMBER 47

Network

There's an old saying, "it's not what you know, it's who you know". This is as true in construction as it is in any industry. If you are not part of a trade group or association, join one. Go to the events and meetings. Talk about yourself and what you do. When you are on the jobsite you may be spending weeks or even months at the same location. Get to know the people you are working around. Most workers love to take a second to chat with someone rather than doing work. Learn names, say good morning and hello when you see the people you have met. Get on social networking sites liked LinkedIn and join conversations on topics you are interested in. Almost everyone you meet could be a possible connection to your future. Nurture your connections and focus on how you may be able to help that person instead of how they can help you. Maybe you can get them in touch with someone who can help them even if you can't and ideally, they might do the same for you.

One more key component to networking I want to mention is; don't burn bridges. This one is important. Everyone I have ever worked for would hire me again and I am proud of that. It has also kept me continuously employed throughout my whole career. It has led to new opportunities and is the reason I am employed in my current position. I worked with the company I am with now several years ago and I quit to go after another opportunity. I left gracefully and explained my reasons. They understood and wished me luck. After about a year, they called me and wanted to know if I was open to coming back but in a new higher paying position. Remember to always operate in a professional manner and never burn bridges. People will remember how you treated them.

NUMBER 48

Bring your Lunch

Most construction companies give you 30 minutes for lunch, at least in the beginning of your career. That's not a lot of time, especially depending on where your jobsite is located. By the time you walk to your truck, drive to the restaurant, wait in the drive-thru, pay, and then drive back, you'll be lucky to have any time to actually eat. Not to mention you are so busy during your break it hardly feels like a break at all. Even though most crews will give you a few minutes here and there, you don't want to be known as the person who is always taking a long lunch. This can also be a time to talk with your coworkers about things other than work (although work often comes up). Lunch may very well be the best time to learn new things about the people you work with.

When packing, bring plenty of water and some sources of protein. Until you learn a jobsite, you'll want to bring food items that can be eaten straight from your lunch box. On bigger jobs, someone will usually bring in a microwave and that can open up a ton of new options. Look online for ideas, there are a plethora of websites devoted to construction lunch ideas.

NUMBER 49

Maintain a Positive Attitude

We've all heard this before. This is standard advice for almost everything that you do and construction is no different. Benefits include; better health, self-esteem, improves teamwork, less sick days, increased productivity, stress reduction, better achievement of goals and career success, more energy and so on. I could go on and on about the benefits on maintaining a positive attitude at work. Being positive won't necessarily make you better at your job, but it will improve the way others view you as a person. This will improve the chances that people will want to help you succeed in your career. At the very least, positivity is infectious and will rub off on your co-workers and facilitate a work environment that is more pleasant to work in. You've heard the phrase, "misery loves company", but so does positivity. Be conscious of the way you interact, if you find yourself being negative, change it. I know you may be thinking this is just a throw away tip, but take a minute to look up some of the science behind being positive. The results are astounding! I am a naturally happy and positive person and I have annoyed others on occasion by refusing to join in on discussions where everyone just sits around and complains, but it wasn't always easy. I do know for sure that my attitude has helped me in my career. Even now, in my last yearly assessment, the owner of our company thanked me for my positive outlook and ability to be to not let the stress of the job bring me down. He then gave me a raise!

NUMBER 50

Try to Learn at Least One New Thing Every day

This doesn't have to be hard and can even be fun. You can start by mastering your tape measure and practicing adding and subtracting fractions. You can learn new ways to utilize your speed square. You could learn how to quickly estimate the ceiling tile needed to install a room. The possibilities are endless. If you do this every day, eventually you will acquire a ton of knowledge that will help you in your career.

I started this tradition when I was an apprentice and an old-timer thought it would be funny to play a small prank on me. We were hanging sheets of 8' drywall and I was acting as the "cut man". A couple guys were up on a scaffold and would yell dimensions to me. I would then walk around the corner to a larger room where our drywall was stacked, cut it, and then bring it back. So, they yelled down to me to cut them a sheet 100" long. I walked over to the drywall pulled my tape and realized that 8' drywall was only 96" long. When I walked back over to the guys they were rolling with laughter at my expense. They knew that 8' was only 96" and wanted to show me how much I still needed to learn. That was the first fact I quickly memorized and I repeated everyday so that I could learn and also avoid being the brunt of another joke.

This strategy has served me well over the years. I became the guy my coworkers would ask to settle a debate on how they should install something or the guy who would know how much a square of shingles is. Not a bad reputation to have. I guess if I think about it, I've morphed into an old-timer. If you are someone who bought this book, you are likely the type of person who also enjoys learning. If you don't know how to go about it, start by learning one new thing a day.

CONCLUSION

I cannot think of a better time than right now to start a career in construction. The massive growth projections coupled with the current labor shortage puts you in the driver's seat of your future. Many industries are in fear that technology will make their jobs obsolete. In construction, the industry fears that technology will increase the need for more workers to use and apply new technologies. Other industries have unhappy workforces and low job satisfaction. Construction workers are among the happiest employees compared to all other industries. How many other professionals can point to a hospital, a road, or a school and say, "I helped build that"? The things you work on will matter to your community.

Construction is rewarding and you will physically see immediate results of your actions. Every day is different and will bring new and exciting challenges.

As I've discussed throughout this book, there are many roles and opportunities available in construction. I really feel that "the sky is the limit". The old perception of the dirty construction worker in his flannel shirt is just that; old (even though you will still find quite a bit of flannel). Construction could very well be the next premier industry with more innovation created than that of Silicon Valley. If you bought this book you are likely thinking about getting into the industry or currently getting started in it. You will determine how far you go. I started out at 13 years old sweeping floors and I now provide a great income for my myself and my family. I did this all without a college degree and you can to! I hope this book will help you in your journey.